Exploring the World of the
AZTECS

with Elaine Landau

Enslow Elementary

an imprint of

Enslow Publishers, Inc.

40 Industrial Road	PO Box 38
Box 398	Aldershot
Berkeley Heights, NJ 07922	Hants GU12 6BP
USA	UK

http://www.enslow.com

Enslow Elementary, an imprint of Enslow Publishers, Inc.

Enslow Elementary ® is a registered trademark of Enslow Publishers, Inc.

Library of Congress Cataloging-in-Publication Data

Landau, Elaine.
    Exploring the world of the Aztecs with Elaine Landau / Elaine Landau.
        p. cm. — (Exploring ancient civilizations with Elaine Landau)
    Includes bibliographical references and index.
    ISBN 0-7660-2341-9
    1. Aztecs—History—Juvenile literature. 2. Aztecs—Social life and customs—
Juvenile literature. I. Title. II. Series
    F1219.73.L35 2005
    972—dc22

                              2004024903

Printed in the United States of America

10 9 8 7 6 5 4 3 2 1

To Our Readers: We have done our best to make sure all Internet addresses in this book were active and appropriate when we went to press. However, the author and the publisher have no control over and assume no liability for the material available on those Internet sites or on other Web sites they may link to. Any comments or suggestions can be sent by e-mail to comments@enslow.com or to the address on the back cover.

All illustrations of Elaine and Max are by © David Pavelonis unless otherwise noted.

Illustration Credits: ©Alison Wright/The Image Works, p. 40 (bottom); ©ARPL / HIP / The Image Works, p.7; ©Clipart.com, pp. 4, 9, 10 (inset), 13 (bottom), 19 (bottom), 25(inset), 30, 36, 46(top); ©Corel Corporation, pp. 11, 17, 20, 24, (top), 25, 27, 28(top), 30, 31(top), 41(middle, left); Library of Congress, pp. 6, 7, 8, 12, 13(top), 15, 21, 31(top), 34(bottom, right); National Cancer Institute, p. 37 (top); ©Painetworks.com, pp. 10 (main), 33(top), 38; ©Photos.com, pp. 41 (top, both), 46 (bottom); Rivera, Diego (1866-1957) © Banco de Mexico Trust. The Great City of Tenochtitlán, 1945. Detail of mural, 4.92 x 9.71 m. Patio Corridor, Location: National Palace, Mexico City, DY., Mexico. Photo Credit Schalkwijk / Art Resource, NY, pp. 42, 43; ©Sean Sprague / The Image Works, p. 32; ©The British Library / HIP / The Image Works, p. 28(bottom), 39 (top); ©The British Museum / HIP / The Image Works, pp.i (Sandstone seated figure of Mictlantecuhtli, Aztec, Mexico, c1325-c1521), ii (Pottery vessel of the Storm God, Teotihuacan, Mexico, c150 BC-AD 750); 13 (left, top), 16, 19(top), 22, 24 (bottom), 26, 29(top), 31 (bottom), 40 (top, right); ©TongRo Image Stock, p. 23; ©Topham /The Image Works , p. 35, 37(bottom).

Front Cover Illustrations: ©Painetworks, Aztec calendar (top, right); ©The British Museum / HIP / The Image Works, Detail of a turquoise mosaic of a double-headed serpent, Aztec/Mixtec, Mexico, 15th-16th century (bottom, right); ©Sean Sprague / The Image Works Tequisquiapan, Queretaro, Mexico: Aztec Dancer (main image).

Back Cover Illustrations: ©The British Museum / HIP / The Image Works, Artist: Unknown. Pottery vessel, Cholula, Mexico, c1200-c1521.

Contents

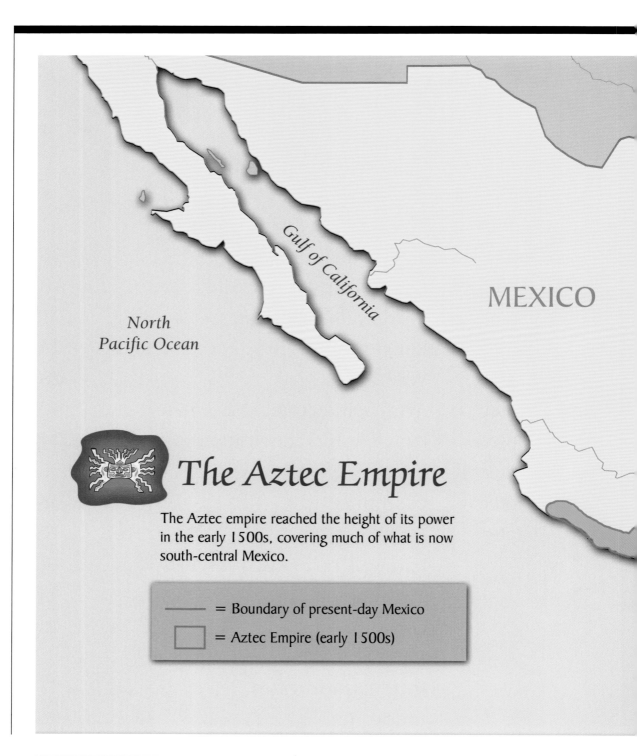

North
Pacific Ocean

Gulf of California

MEXICO

The Aztec Empire

The Aztec empire reached the height of its power in the early 1500s, covering much of what is now south-central Mexico.

————	= Boundary of present-day Mexico
☐	= Aztec Empire (early 1500s)

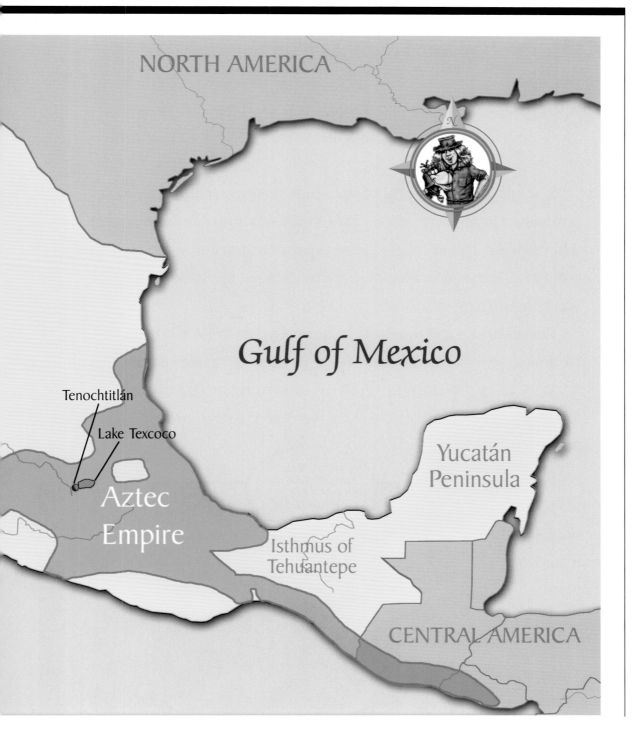

NORTH AMERICA

Gulf of Mexico

Tenochtitlán

Lake Texcoco

Aztec Empire

Yucatán Peninsula

Isthmus of Tehuantepe

CENTRAL AMERICA

Dear Fellow Explorer,

If you could travel back in time, where would you go? Would you want to visit an ancient civilization?

The place I have in mind had huge palaces, sculptures, and temples. There were large cities with bustling marketplaces. The people living there were great engineers and town planners. They were special in many other ways as well. They were the Aztecs.

I am Elaine Landau and this is my dog, Max. We are about to travel five hundred years back in time. We are going to Mexico to get a close-up view of the Aztecs. The trip was Max's idea. He heard the Aztecs were very interesting people. Now he wants to see for himself. Why not join us? You don't need to pack— just turn the page!

THAT'S RIGHT, MAX. TENOCHTITLÁN HAS BEEN DESCRIBED AS THE "GARDEN OF THE WORLD."

WOW! THIS IS SOME SUPER CITY. A DOG COULD REALLY HAVE A GREAT TIME HERE WITH ALL THESE PARKS AND TREES.

The ruins of Tenochtitlán lie under the buildings of modern day Mexico City. An idea of the beauty of the city may be seen in this drawing. It shows Aztec warriors defending the temple of Tenochtitlán. The warriors are fighting off attackers who can be seen dead on the ground.

History

Early on, the Aztecs, or Mexicas as they were known, were nomads. This means they moved from place to place. In the mid-1200s, they came to the Valley of Mexico. This valley was about forty miles wide and surrounded by tall mountains.

In the valley there were many small city-states. Each was a little country centered around a single city with stone houses, gardens, and farming areas. The valley was beautiful but not peaceful. The different city-states were often at war with one another.

The Aztecs were not always welcome in the valley because they were fierce fighters. Their new neighbors found them warlike and menacing. But they also found that the

According to legend, the god Huitzilopochtli (wee-tsee-lo-POCH-tlee) told the Aztecs to build their city, Tenochtitlán, on the spot where an eagle landed on a cactus.

Aztecs could be useful. The different city-states often hired them to fight their enemies.

When not being paid to fight, the Aztecs continued to roam. They wandered throughout central Mexico. Then in the early fourteenth century, they found a home of their own. They settled in the southern end of the Valley of Mexico. There they built their city on the swampy island of Tenochtitlán (te-noch-TEE-tlan). This was an island in the center of Lake Texcoco (tesh-KO-ko).

The Aztecs began building their fabulous city in 1325.

The Aztecs built their capital city on an island, so they had to build special types of bridges called causeways to get to the mainland. The center of Tenochtitlán included a large temple area surrounded by palaces.

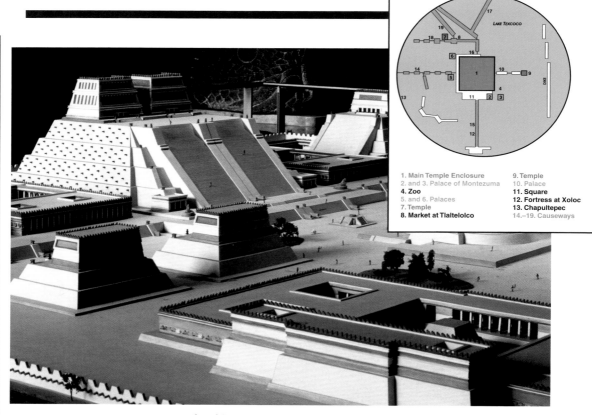

Tenochtitlán may have looked like this.

1. Main Temple Enclosure
2. and 3. Palace of Montezuma
4. Zoo
5. and 6. Palaces
7. Temple
8. Market at Tlaltelolco
9. Temple
10. Palace
11. Square
12. Fortress at Xoloc
13. Chapultepec
14.–19. Causeways

It covered up two thirds of the island and was also named Tenochtitlán. The city of Tenochtitlán was larger than most European cities at that time. About two hundred fifty thousand people lived there. On the north end of the island, the Aztecs built a second city named Tlatelolco (tla-te-LOL-ko). It was known for its large, busy marketplace.

Building on the island had not been easy. The Aztecs had to drain the marshes (swamp areas). They had to make channels, or canals, throughout the island. People used canoes in these canals to travel to different places. The Aztecs also built stone causeways to connect their island to the mainland. A causeway is a raised roadway.

Tenochtitlán was located near two other powerful city-states. To the east were the Aeolhuaca (A-kol-WA-ka) of Texcoco. To the west were the Tepaneca (te-pan-E-ka) of Tlacopán (tla-KO-pan). The Aztecs formed alliances, or friendships, with both of these city-states. This made the Aztecs even more powerful. The alliance between Tenochtitlán, Texcoco, and Tlacopán became known as the Triple Alliance.

As time passed, the Aztecs began conquering by moving into the surrounding territories. By about 1450, they had an empire that included much of central Mexico.

The Aztecs ruled their empire forcefully. They had a strong and well-trained army. For most of the fifteenth century, they rarely lost on the battlefield.

Spanish cathedrals were built on Aztec ruins.

The Year the Spanish Arrived

*E*verything changed for the Aztecs in 1519. That year the Spanish explorer Hernando Cortés came to Mexico from the island of Cuba. Cortés had a small band of explorers with him. They came in search of gold and other riches. Cortés soon learned that the Aztecs had both.

When Cortés and his men reached the city, they were amazed by the Aztecs' achievements. Bernal Diaz del Castillo was one of the men in Cortés' group. Diaz described the "spacious and well built" Aztec palaces. He felt that they were "all a wonder to behold."

Montezuma II had become the emperor of the Aztecs in 1502. He was ruling when Cortés arrived. Some historians think that at first Montezuma did not resist the invaders because he believed Cortés was a returning god. Later, Montezuma tried to make the

Hernando Cortés was a Spanish conquistador. In Spanish, *conquistador* means "conqueror."

Montezuma II was one of the greatest emperors of the Aztec people.

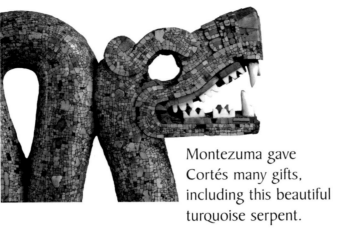

Montezuma gave Cortés many gifts, including this beautiful turquoise serpent.

x altelolco.

This drawing shows Cortés (seated) being welcomed by Montezuma in Tenochtitlán. The woman next to Cortés is Dona Maria, a non-Aztec Mexican who came from the area where the Spanish landed. She learned Spanish quickly and became Cortés' translator, making conversation possible between Cortés and Montezuma.

Spaniards leave. He threatened them. He also tried to convince them to go peacefully. He even gave the Spaniards gifts. These included many items made with rare and beautiful feathers.

Before long, however, Cortés and his men took Montezuma prisoner. They wanted to take over the city of Tenochtitlán. In May 1520 the Aztecs rebelled and fought the invaders. Montezuma died. Some historians think he may have died from wounds he received while fighting. Others believe that the Spaniards murdered him.

In any case, the Aztecs won. Two thirds of the Spaniards were killed. The rest were driven from the city in June 1520.

However, in May 1521, Cortés returned with hundreds of Spanish soldiers. Cortés had also formed alliances with groups of other Mexican Indians. These were the Aztecs' enemies. Tens of thousands of them now marched with the Spaniards.

The Aztecs fought their attackers for three months. But the Spaniards destroyed their causeways. This cut the Aztecs off from the mainland. They began to run out of food and water.

In the end the Spaniards won. Many Aztecs were killed. Their beautiful city lay in ruins. The remains of Tenochtitlán belonged to the conquerors.

In the years that followed, increasing numbers of Spaniards arrived. By 1535 all of Mexico was a Spanish colony. Mexico City, the capital of Mexico, is now built on the same spot as Tenochtitlán.

Although the Spanish settlers tried to destroy the Aztecs' way of life, much of their culture survived. People still study their civilization today.

The Spaniards and the Aztecs fought fiercely. In the end the Aztecs were defeated.

3 Government

*T*he Aztec emperor was a very powerful man. He was known as Huey Tlatoani (tla-KOT-tlee), or "Great Speaker." It meant that he represented, or spoke for all Aztecs.

Next in power after the emperor was his second in command. Though he was always a man, his title was Snake Woman. He helped the emperor run the empire. Snake Woman was also the name of a goddess.

The title of emperor was not always passed from father to son. Instead, a group of four nobles called the Tlatocan (tla-TO-can) chose the new emperor. These nobles came from important families. All were related to the first Aztec ruler.

When an emperor died, the Tlatocan picked another ruler. It might be the son or brother of the dead ruler. The council always chose a person who had proved himself in battle. Bravery was very important to the Aztecs.

The Aztecs had three levels of nobles. At the highest level were the

The emperor's second in command was called Snake Woman. The snake was a very important animal to the Aztecs. Many of their gods were shown as snakes, as represented in this Aztec carving of a rattlesnake.

tlatoque (tla-TO-que). This was the ruling class. Aztec emperors came from this class. So did the men who governed large Aztec cities. The next highest level of Aztec nobles was the tetecutin (te-TEK' W-teen). They governed smaller areas than those in the ruling class. The third level of nobles was the pipiltin. They often held government positions. Some were Aztec priests.

The Aztecs believed in law and order. Very serious crimes were tried in a court in Tenochtitlán. Punishments could be harsh. In some cases, people were sentenced to death for stealing. They could also be put to death for being drunk in public. The Aztecs did not have prisons.

To oversee the rest of the empire, the Aztecs in Tenochtitlán sometimes sent soldiers to rebellious areas. At times, traders served as spies for the emperor as well.

Aztec society had different levels of nobles, like a pyramid. The tlatoque were at the top, the tetecutin in the middle, and pipiltin on the bottom level.

Society and Family Life

No Aztec was more important than the emperor. His subjects were not even allowed to look directly at him.

Next in rank were the nobles. There were also ordinary, or common, people. A person's importance did not depend on how much money he or she had. The family one belonged to was what mattered. Some commoners were even richer than nobles!

All Aztecs were members of territorial groups known as calpulli (kal-PO-lee). Each calpulli worked an amount of farmland. The various families in a calpulli farmed a portion of this land each year.

IT LOOKS LIKE THE AZTECS WERE HARD WORKERS.

THAT'S TRUE. THE AZTECS DISLIKED LAZINESS. THEY BEGAN WORK AT SUNRISE EVERY DAY.

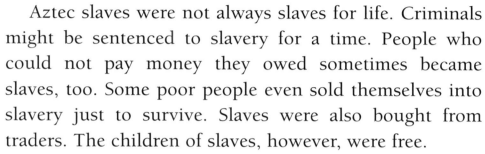

Aztecs sometimes made pottery to sell at the marketplace.

Often Aztec nobles owned even more land. This was given to them by the emperor. It was a reward for their services. Nobles had slaves to do the work for them in the fields.

Aztec slaves were not always slaves for life. Criminals might be sentenced to slavery for a time. People who could not pay money they owed sometimes became slaves, too. Some poor people even sold themselves into slavery just to survive. Slaves were also bought from traders. The children of slaves, however, were free.

Family life was important to the Aztecs. Every family member had a job to do. Husbands were expected to support their wives and children. Some men were soldiers, potters, or wood-carvers. Others were metalworkers or stone workers. Wives cooked, cleaned, made clothing, and cared for their children. Women sometimes made pottery, too. They sold their goods in the marketplace.

WOOD-CARVER   WEAVER

FISHERMEN   SPINNERS

Young girls learned how to take care of a home. Some daughters from noble families were educated. They went to temple schools run by priests and they studied to become priestesses.

Boys learned to farm and fish. If their fathers were craftsmen, they learned a craft. Most Aztec boys went to school, too. The children of commoners studied history, religion, and war. The boys were taught how to use weapons and win battles. When they were older, they would be called on to serve as soldiers.

The sons of nobles did not have to join the military. They attended different schools. They learned to read and write. They also studied math and law. Many of them later became judges, priests, and government officials.

Boys and girls who became priests or priestesses could enter sacred parts of the temples. The Temple of the Moon (below) was built long before the Aztecs, in the ancient city of Teotihuacan. The Aztecs later took over the area that held the city.

World of Work

Many Aztecs farmed. Corn was their major crop. They also grew beans, squash, tomatoes, chilies, avocados, and sweet potatoes.

There were few farmers in the city of Tenochtitlán itself. Priests, craftspeople, and government officials worked there. Farming was done in the areas surrounding Aztec cities.

To add to their land, the Aztecs used chinampas (chee-NAM-paz). These were crop islands created in the lake near their island city of Tenochtitlán.

Chinampas are often called floating gardens. However, they do not actually float but are anchored to the bottom of the lake by trees.

The islands were made by digging up mud from the bottom of the lake. The mud was placed on straw mats on the water's surface. The Aztecs planted trees on the corners of these islands. The tree roots grew down to the lake's bottom and anchored the islands. The Aztecs grew many different crops on chinampas.

Trade was also very important to the Aztecs. Thousands of people came to their busy marketplaces. Farmers came to sell their crops, and craftsmen came to sell their goods. Doctors treated patients and barbers even cut hair there!

The Aztecs often used a special kind of light blue stone called turquoise. This mask was made by embedding pieces of turquoise into a human skull.

There were also traveling merchants, who carried goods throughout the empire. They traded what they brought for things that people in other places might need.

All conquered people had to pay tribute to the emperor. The government had tax collectors that went to the different regions to collect what was due to the emperor.

The Aztecs did not use money, though sometimes cocoa beans were used in its place. Usually tribute was paid with crops, cloth, bundles of feathers, dyes, woven cotton blankets, shields, gold, copper, jade, and other items of value.

A modern-day mural in Mexico City shows what the marketplace in Tenochtitlán might have looked like.

eligion was a very important part of life for the Aztecs. They worshipped numerous gods and goddesses. There were gods for different crops. People working in jobs prayed to their own special gods as well.

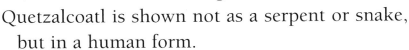

This carving of Quetzalcoatl shows the god's snake head surrounded by feathers.

Among the Aztecs' gods was Quetzalcoatl (ket-tsal-KO-atl)— the feathered serpent. Despite his name, in some drawings, Quetzalcoatl is shown not as a serpent or snake, but in a human form.

Tlaloc (tal-lok), the rain god, was highly valued by the Aztecs. Long droughts could kill crops. When this happened, people starved. So the Aztecs were anxious to please Tlaloc. Tezcatlipoca (tes-ka-lee-PO-ka) was the Aztecs'

This stone figure of Tlaloc was found by scientists at the site of one of the god's shrines. The Aztecs often made such figures and placed them as offerings at the shrines.

most important god. Tezcatlipoca was the god of creation, rulership, and warfare.

Another important god to the people of Tenochtitlán was Huitzilopochtli (wee-tsee-lo-POCH-tlee). His name means "Hummingbird on the Left." The Aztecs believed that Huitzilopochtli led them to their island home in the Valley of Mexico. Huitzilopochtli was their main god of war. The Aztecs looked to him for victory in battle. He was also one of their sun gods.

Humans were killed or sacrificed to please some gods. This was part of the

A construction crew in Mexico City found this Aztec altar when they were digging for a subway. Aztecs made sacrifices on altars like this.

THIS IS PRETTY GRISLY. YOU KNOW, THEY SACRIFICED DOGS AS WELL AS PEOPLE.

YES, BUT BIRDS WERE THE ANIMALS MOST OFTEN SACRIFICED.

Aztec religion. It was done for Huitzilopochtli, Tlaloc, and other gods. The Aztecs believed these gods wanted human hearts and blood.

The Aztecs felt that without sacrifices the gods would be angry. They might cause a drought or famine. At worst, they might end the world.

War captives were sacrificed to please Huitzilopochtli. Aztec soldiers would lead their captives up to the altar to die. Sometimes, the Aztecs sacrificed their own people as well. Being sacrificed to a god was considered an honor. Child victims were sacrificed to the god Tlaloc.

Aztec priests performed these sacrifices. They were done in front of large crowds.

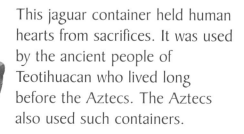

This jaguar container held human hearts from sacrifices. It was used by the ancient people of Teotihuacan who lived long before the Aztecs. The Aztecs also used such containers.

The priest would cut out the victim's heart. Then he would hold it up to the people.

In a single year, thousands of people may have been killed this way. Only the victim's head would be kept. The rest of the body would be thrown away.

However, there was more to the Aztecs' religion than sacrifices. The Aztecs performed religious ceremonies in their homes and in public to honor different gods. Sometimes there was feasting at the public ceremonies. Very brave soldiers might be rewarded there as well.

This Aztec skull rack, part of the ruins of the sacrificial altar of Templo Mayor, was discovered under Mexico City. The skulls of sacrificial victims were placed on the skull rack. These victims were mostly war captives sacrificed to honor the gods.

War

War was part of the Aztecs' way of life. They often went to war to take captives needed as sacrifices to their gods. War also brought the Aztecs wealth. A captured city would have to keep paying tribute or taxes to the emperor.

Just like the animal, Aztec jaguar warriors were fierce fighters.

The Aztec army officers were usually nobles. However, some commoners who fought bravely and took many captives were often rewarded. Some were made army officers, positions normally held by nobles. It was the only way a common person could enjoy some of the privileges nobles had.

Aztec warriors carried one or two wooden throwing spears into battle.

This pottery figurine of an eagle warrior was used by Aztecs when they worshipped at home.

Some very brave soldiers became members of the eagle or jaguar order of soldiers. These were very fierce fighters. The jaguar order wore jaguar skins. The eagle order had helmets that looked like the eagle. They wore a feathered covering as well. These were thickly padded with cotton. They served as armor against their enemies' spears and arrows. Soldiers in the jaguar and eagle orders were highly respected. They were often given the honor of leading Aztec armies into battle.

Aztec soldiers were known for their bravery. When Cortés and his men fought the Aztecs, their courage in battle amazed the Spaniards. As one Spaniard wrote about the Aztec fighters: "They sprang upon us like lions."

Art, Architecture, and Science

The Aztecs were skilled architects. They designed and built magnificent temples for their gods. The most outstanding one was the Great Temple at Tenochtitlán. The Great Temple was the center of Aztec religious life. Most of the human sacrifices were performed there.

This temple was nine stories high. It was a large pyramid with two sets of steps to the top. Atop the Great Temple were two impressive shrines. These were for the Aztec gods Huitzilopochtli and Tlaloc. The shrines were decorated with carvings and paintings. Inside them were statues of these two gods. Sculptors also created statues of people and animals placed elsewhere in the city.

Architecture and art were important to the Aztecs. They had many great artisans. Jewelry makers worked with

Though only parts of the Great Temple exist today, the whole building can be seen at the left of this drawing. In the foreground, a causeway leads up to Tenochtitlán.

These statues lean against the inner steps of the Aztec temple, Templo Mayor.

gold and copper. They fashioned pendants as well as ear, lip, and nose jewelry. Other metalworkers made attractive wall panels.

Artisans who worked with feathers were highly respected. Colorful feathers were used in headdresses, cloaks, and shields worn by nobles. Items made with blue-green feathers were the most valuable. These were the tail feathers of the Guatemalan quetzal bird.

Aztec artists made beautiful mosaics as well. These were patterns or designs made with small colorful pieces of stones. Craftsmen would often use imported turquoise for this. The Aztecs created mosaic masks, shields, and statues.

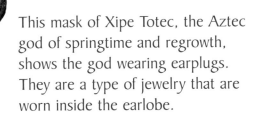

This mask of Xipe Totec, the Aztec god of springtime and regrowth, shows the god wearing earplugs. They are a type of jewelry that are worn inside the earlobe.

Artists who worked with feathers often made headdresses. This modern Aztec dancer wears a fancy headdress.

Some Aztec craftsmen were known for their outstanding stonework. Aztec potters were busy, too. They made plates, bowls, and jugs.

Poetry was another valued Aztec art. Usually poetry was recited aloud in front of groups of people. The best Aztec poets were admired. People often learned their poems by heart. They taught these to their children. This is an Aztec poem about war:

There is nothing like death in war;
Nothing like flowery death.
So precious to him who gives life:
Far off I see it, my heart yearns for it.

Some Aztecs were interested in science. Aztec doctors used plants and herbs to help treat different illnesses. They were also used for poisonous snake bites.

The Aztecs were interested in astronomy, too. They studied the movements of the stars and planets. The Aztecs used these movements to determine the passage of time.

To help them keep track of time, the Aztecs created two calendars. One was the solar calendar. This calendar

Time was very important to the Aztecs. One of their calendars was divided into eighteen months of twenty days each.

was divided the year into 365 days. It had eighteen months. Each month was made up of twenty days. Five days were left over. These were not included in any month. They were believed to be unlucky days.

The solar calendar was tied to the crop-growing season. It was used to set marketplace days and special festivals.

The other Aztec calendar was made up of 260 days. These were broken up into twenty separate periods. Each period had thirteen days. The Aztecs used this calendar to determine the right days to go to battle.

WOW! THIS AZTEC CALENDAR STONE IS A REALLY HUGE SCULPTURE.

THAT'S RIGHT, MAX. IT'S OVER THIRTEEN FEET WIDE AND WEIGHS NEARLY TWENTY-FIVE TONS!

Housing in Tenochtitlán

enochtitlán was a splendid city. The Great Temple stood near the center of Tenochtitlán. Close by were other temples, schools, courts of law, and the emperor's palaces. Trees and colorful flowers were planted everywhere. There were wading pools, too.

The most magnificent building in the city was the emperor's main palace. This was a huge structure with

Montezuma's palace was in the center of Tenochtitlán. His personal bodyguard of 200 chieftains stayed in the room next to his.

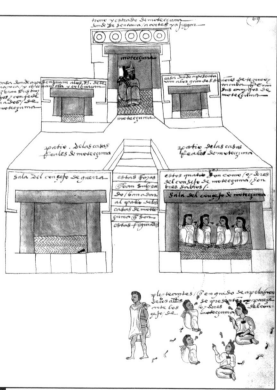

courtyards and gardens. The palace had guest rooms, and servants' living quarters, as well as government offices. The emperor and his family lived in a separate private area of the palace.

Emperor Montezuma kept his own zoo on the grounds. It had hundreds of colorful birds. There were also jaguars, monkeys, bears, and other animals.

Of all the buildings the ancient Aztecs made, mostly only pyramids still stand today. Only the foundations remain of other Aztec buildings.

Wealthy Aztec nobles also lived well. They had big homes, usually made of whitewashed stone. The white color reflected the sunlight. This helped keep their homes cool in the summer.

In the center of these homes were open courtyards with well-tended gardens and sitting areas. Many also had flat roofs where people grew lovely gardens.

Middle-class and poorer people had smaller homes. These homes were usually made of adobe, or sun-dried mud bricks. Others were made of wattle and daub, a blend of sticks woven together and mud. These houses had no windows so most people spent time outside on their patios.

Food

The Aztecs ate a variety of foods. Each day a team of chefs prepared over three hundred different dishes for Emperor Montezuma. The emperor could choose whatever he wanted. The choices usually included turkey, quail, duck, wild boar, and rabbit.

Montezuma liked to finish his meal with a cold chocolate drink, served in a solid gold goblet. He usually had his cocoa spiced with chili peppers or other flavors.

Wealthy nobles often had a choice of dishes, too. They ate more meats and imported foods than commoners. They often ate turkey or duck stew and a variety of fish.

Both nobles and commoners ate vegetables, too. Tomatoes, corn, squash, peppers, and beans were among the vegetables eaten.

Corn was an important food for commoners. They flavored and prepared it in different ways. Usually they made slim cornmeal

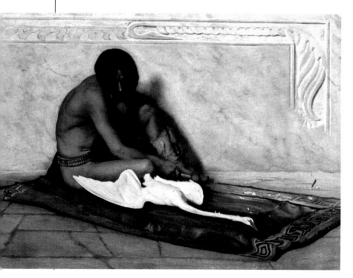

An Aztec man prepares a bird to be eaten.

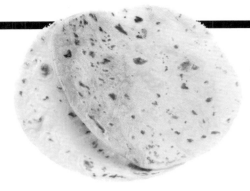

Tortillas

Tamales

pancakes. We call these tortillas. The Aztecs also used corn to make gruel, a soft food, by boiling cornmeal in water.

On special occasions, commoners had tamales, a meat dish seasoned with spices and wrapped in husks and cooked. The Aztecs often flavored their foods with chili peppers and natural herbs and spices as well.

This is a statue of an Aztec maize, or corn, god. The priest of this god wore the skins of the people the Aztecs sacrificed. Wearing the victims' skins represented the rebirth of crops.

Clothing

Aztecs of different classes wore clothing of different materials. A commoner's garments were made of rough cloth, usually made from the desert maguey or yucca plant.

The men wore loincloths. This was a length of material drawn up between a man's legs and tied with a knot in front. Aztec men also wore cloaks draped around their shoulders. The cloaks of commoners were plain. They were not dyed and were not permitted to reach below the knees. Longer cloaks were only for nobles.

Aztec women wore long loose-fitting blouses. They draped material around their hips to form a skirt. It was tied on with a belt.

The nobles wore the same clothing items as commoners, except theirs were made of cotton. Usually the cloth was

These modern Aztec dancers wear traditional Aztec clothing.

Aztec men wore loincloths. They also wore decorated capes held in place by a knot over the shoulder. Most women wore wraparound skirts with a belt.

dyed bright colors. Reds, purples, greens, and blues were typical. Often the cloaks of nobles were beautifully embroidered. Some had feathers woven into them. Special designs on the cloak showed the person's rank. Noblewomen had beautifully embroidered skirts and blouses, too.

Nobles also wore a lot of jewelry. These were often set with gemstones. The highest nobles and officials wore golden headbands, pendants, and ear, nose, and lip jewelry.

Heading Home

The Aztecs had an outstanding civilization. They built beautiful cities. They made important contributions in the fields of arts and sciences. We even use some words from their spoken language of Nahuatl (NA-watl). The words tomato and guacamole come from the Aztecs.

This statue represents the Aztec water goddess, Chalchiuhtlicue (chal-CHEE-uh-TLEE-cue).

The Temple of the Sun at Teotihuacan, Mexico, was once on land that was part of the giant Aztec empire.

Tomatoes

Guacamole

These carvings of Tlaloc, the rain god of the Aztecs, can be found on the Jaguar Temple in Mexico.

Seeing the Aztec world was great. But now it is time to go home. We are glad you came along with us. Time travel is always more fun with friends. To the time machine!

IT'S A SHAME TENOCHTITLÁN NO LONGER EXISTS. I BET LOTS OF PEOPLE WOULD LIKE TO SEE IT.

WELL, MAX, THEY CAN ALWAYS READ ABOUT THE AZTECS AND COME TIME TRAVELING WITH US.

This is how a modern artist, Diego Rivera, depicted life in the Aztec capital city, Tenochtitlán. Rivera was a Mexican artist famous for murals that portrayed the life and history of Mexico. Look for things in the mural that relate to Aztec life.

Farewell Fellow Explorer,

I just wanted to take a moment to tell you a little about the real "Max and me." I am a children's book author and Max is a small, fluffy white dog. I almost named him Marshmallow because of how he looked. However, he seems to think he's human—so only a more dignified name would do. Max also seems to think that he is a large, powerful dog. He fearlessly chases after much larger dogs in the neighborhood. Max was thrilled when the artist for this book drew him as a dog several times his size. He felt that someone in the art world had finally captured his true spirit.

In real life, Max is quite a traveler. I have taken him to nearly every state while doing research for different books. We live in Florida so when we go north I have to pack a sweater for him. When we were in Oregon it rained and I was glad I brought his raincoat. None of this gear is necessary when time traveling. My "take-off" spot is the computer station and as always Max sits faithfully by my side.

Best Wishes,
Elaine & Max (a small dog with big dreams)

Timeline

Mid-1200s	The Aztecs come to the Valley of Mexico.
1325	The city of Tenochtitlán is founded.
1428	The Triple Alliance is formed.
1440	Montezuma I becomes emperor.
1440–1469	Triple Alliance conquers large areas to the south and east.
1450	Tenochtitlán becomes a major city. It is as large as many European cities of its time.
1469	Montezuma I dies.
1473	Aztecs conquer city of Tlatelolco.
1487	The Aztecs complete building the Great Temple at Tenochtitlán.
1502	Montezuma II becomes emperor.
1519	Spanish explorer Hernando Cortés comes to Mexico.
1520	The Aztecs rebel against the Spanish invaders. They drive the Spaniards out of Tenochtitlán, but Montezuma II is killed.
May 1521	Spanish forces return to Tenochtitlán with thousands of Mexican Indian allies.
August 1521	Aztecs surrender to the Spanish.
1535	All of Mexico becomes a Spanish colony.

Glossary

alliance—A friendship or special bond.

artisan—A skilled craftsperson.

causeway—A raised roadway.

chinampas—Islands created for growing crops.

calpulli—A territorial or land area group.

cocoa beans—Beans from the cacao tree used to make chocolate.

drought—A long period of hot, dry weather.

emperor—Ruler of an empire.

famine—A serious lack of food.

loincloth—A piece of material drawn up between a man's legs and tied with a knot in front.

mosaic—A pattern or design made up of small pieces of colored glass, tile, or stone.

sacrifice—An offering made to a god.

tribute—Goods given to an emperor as a sort of tax.

vessel—A ship or boat.

Further Reading

Ardagh, Peter. *The Aztecs*. New York: Peter Bendrick Books, 2000.

Kimmel, Eric A. *Montezuma and the Fall of the Aztecs*. New York: Holiday House, 2000.

Macdonald, Fiona. *You Wouldn't Want to Be an Aztec Sacrifice!* Danbury, Conn.: Franklin Watts, 2000.

Platt, Richard. *Aztecs: The Fall of the Aztec Capital*. New York: DK Publishing, 1999.

Wyborny, Sheila. *The Aztec Empire*. San Diego, Calif.: Blackbirch, 2003.

Internet Addresses

History of Mexico

<http://www.globalvolunteers.org/1main/mexico/mexicohistory.htm>

Web site on Mexico's history beginning with the Aztecs.

The Aztec Calendar

<http://www.azteccalendar.com/>

Visit this colorful Web site for information on the Aztec calendars.

Index